Recess in the Dark

Poems from the Far North

Written by Kalli Dakos, Illustrated by Erin Mercer

DC Canada Education Publishing

Author: Kalli Dakos

Illustrator: Erin Mercer

Editors: Kara Cybanski, Leonard Judge

Cover Design: Erin Mercer

Published in 2020 by: DC Canada Education Publishing

170 Laurier Ave. West, Suite 603
Ottawa, ON, Canada K1P 5V5
www.dc-canada.ca

Text © 2019 Kalli Dakos
Illustrations © 2019 DC Canada Education Publishing

All rights reserved. No part of this book may be reproduced in any form or by any electronic or mechanical means including information storage and retrieval systems without written permission of the copyright owner.

We acknowledge the financial support of the Government of Canada for our publishing activities..

Recess in the Dark

ISBN: 978-1-77205-429-3

Library and Archives Canada Cataloguing in Publication

Title: Recess in the Dark: Poems from the Far North / by Kalli Dakos; illustrated by Erin Mercer.
Names: Dakos, Kalli, author. | Mercer, Erin, 1986- illustrator.
Identifiers: Canadiana 2019013612X | ISBN 9781772054293 (softcover)
Subjects: LCSH: Arctic regions—Juvenile poetry.
Classification: LCC PS3554.A414 R43 2019 | DDC j811/.6—dc23

Dedication

For Dr. John, Nancy, Sylvia, David, Chipo, Marilyn, Roz and all the others who were in the far north with me, and especially for the students at Sir Alexander Mackenzie School in Inuvik, Northwest Territories, Canada, who inspired these poems and wrote many of their own.

For the children who live in lands where Recess in the Dark is a part of their lives, and for those who will have the opportunity to explore this amazing experience through these poems.

Acknowledgement

I would like to acknowledge my friend, Laura Cinkant, who is always ready and willing to edit my work and give feedback on new manuscripts. I am so thankful for all her help with this book.

Kalli Dakos

A Warning for Wimpy Kids

For wimpy kids,
A WARNING!
Recess here is stark.
It's colder than a freezer,
wild, bleak, and dark.

A smile can stay frozen,
solid on a face,
and frostbite comes with pain
in this frigid northern place.

The moon and stars gaze upon
a land that's bittersweet.
Kids blend into the shadows
with ice beneath their feet.

For wimpy kids, A WARNING
that I'd like to make clear,
Recess in the Dark
is for the strong who live up here.

The Sun Won't Shine

The earth here tilts
in such a way
that night is dark
and so is day.

For several weeks,
the sun won't shine
or reach the north
in wintertime.

On a playground
icy and white,
children have recess
in the dark of night.

There are days in the far north when the sun does not shine and it is dark all the time. The children walk to school in the dark, have recess in the dark, and go home in the dark. In the summer, the reverse happens. There are days when the sun shines all the time and it never gets dark.

Under the Stars

We puff right up
in big snowsuits,
with hats and mitts
and furry boots.

Many layers
of clothing go,
on arms and legs
from head to toe.

Scarves are wrapped
around our faces,
and eyes peer out
from dark places.

We look like
aliens from Mars,
ready to play
under the stars.

In order to stay warm in the cold and dark, children wear many layers of clothing—snowsuits, windpants, sweaters, jackets, parkas, heavy mittens, hats, hoods, scarves, boots, mukluks, etc. A parka is a northern coat that is trimmed in fur, and mukluks are warm, soft boots. The children wear scarves and hats that cover up their entire faces except for their eyes.

We'll Be Your Light

The stars are shimmering and seem to say,

"Come out in the dark and shadows today.

Come play in the cold, this winter's-day-night.

Come out for recess. We'll be your light."

The school has lights on the playground, but it is still pitch-black. At times, the dark northern sky shimmers with stars.

A Raven

A raven soars
way up high,
with black wings
on an Arctic sky.

A mighty bird,
cold-weather-strong,
to stay with us
all winter long.

Most birds fly to warmer climates in the winter, but the raven laughs in the face of the cold winds as if to say, "You can't make me leave."

Hide and Seek in the Dark

You go and hide,
and I will seek.
I promise, Ben,
that I won't peek.

1 2 3 4 5 6 7 8 9 10

Hide and seek
is so much fun
in the shadows
where we run.

It's not the game
we play in light.
It's different in
the dark of night.

Where are you, Ben?
I cannot see.
There's so much dark
surrounding me.

But I'm determined
to find you.
Your bright red mittens
are a clue.

I check the fort,
the swings, the slide.
I wonder where
you went to hide.

I look behind
the snowman too,
and peer inside
the dark igloo.

Come on moon.
Come on stars.
Light the way.
He can't be far.

Riiiiiiiiiiiiiiiiiiiiiiiiiiiiiiiiiiiiiiing!

Recess has come
right to an end,

and the dark
is still hiding Ben.

Hide and seek is a favourite game in the North, especially in the dark. The children use clues like the colour of mittens or scarves to find their friends. Where do you think Ben is?

Lucy and Her Frozen Belly Button

It's soooooooooooooooooooooooooooooooooooo cold,

that my body's turning blue,

and the button

on my belly

is frozen too.

The children dress warmly in the winter, but there are still days when they are cold. I am certain Lucy can hardly wait for the bell to ring so she can go inside.

Icy Slide

Watch us climb
this mountain of snow,
huffing and puffing
as we go.

At the top
there is an icy slide,
a super-scary
dark-night ride.

Zipping down
at the speed of light!
Flashes of snowsuits
in the night!

There are mountains of snow all over the playground and the children climb to the top and slide down them. Sometimes the "slide" is icy, which makes the ride extra fast.

The Northern Lights

The northern lights
put on a show
in the polar sky.
They prance,
they dance,
keep us entranced,
a whirlwind up high.

The colours stream
in blues and greens
with blazing, golden rays.
They light the night
with wild light
across the Milky Way.

We cannot run,
we cannot play,
we cannot even speak.
In a daze,
we just gaze
until our legs go weak.

Faraway we hear the bell,
to call us back inside.
We can't move;
in fact, we're glued
to the wonders in the sky!

People from all over the world visit the North to see the Northern Lights (also called Aurora Borealis). They are magical lights that form amazing, colourful patterns as they swirl and dance in the sky.

Northern Magic

Standing on Snow Mountain
and gazing at the sky,

I imagine
that I am all grown up,

an astronaut,
floating,
gliding,
drifting,
with the moon and the stars,

and looking down
at the polar ice caps,
the Arctic tundra,
a town,
a school,

and a kid,
on Snow Mountain,
gazing up at the sky.

There are mountains of snow in the cold and darkness. It is fun to climb to the top and imagine what it would be like to float with the moon and the stars.

This is a free verse poem. It has its own structure and it does not need to rhyme.

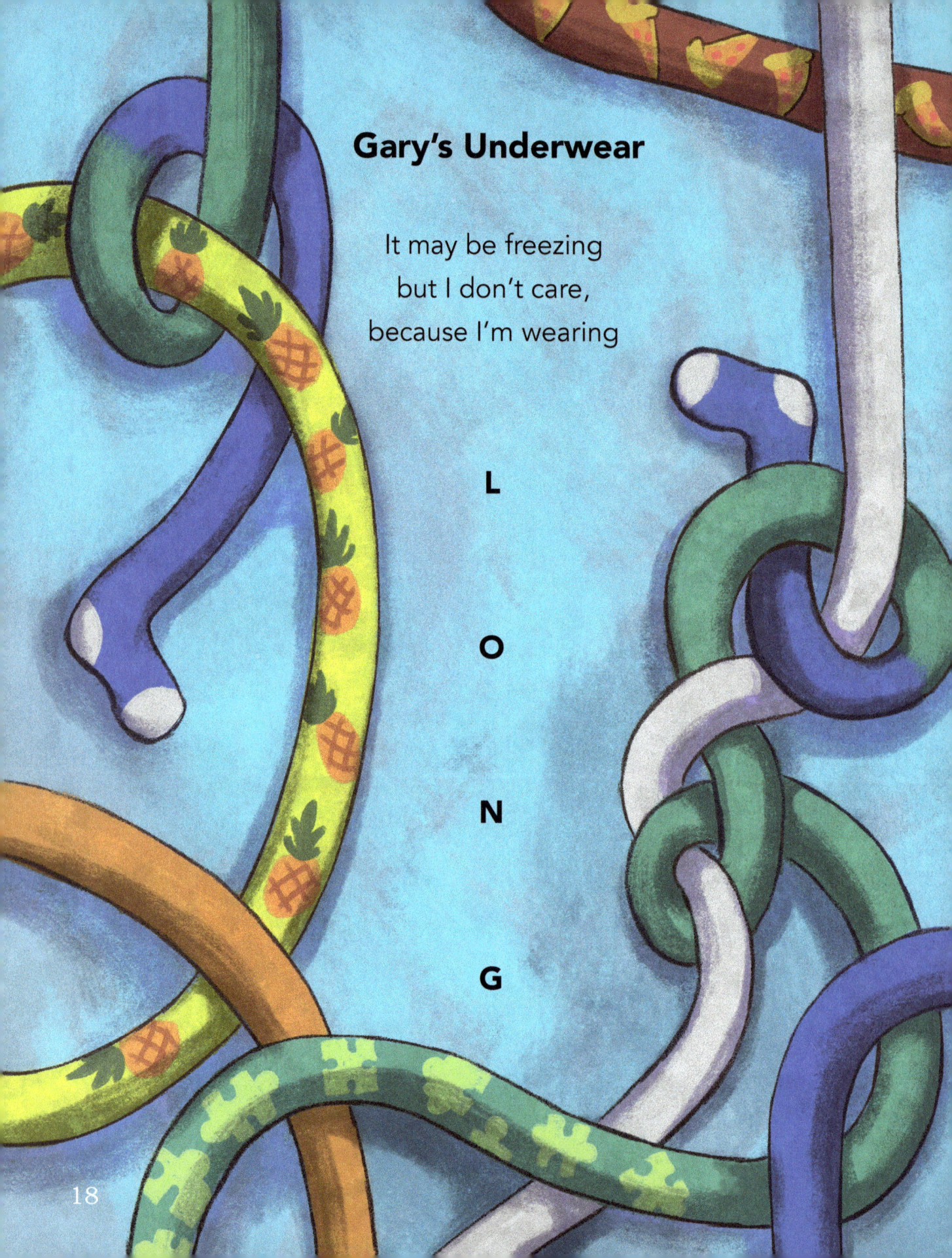

Gary's Underwear

It may be freezing
but I don't care,
because I'm wearing

L

O

N

G

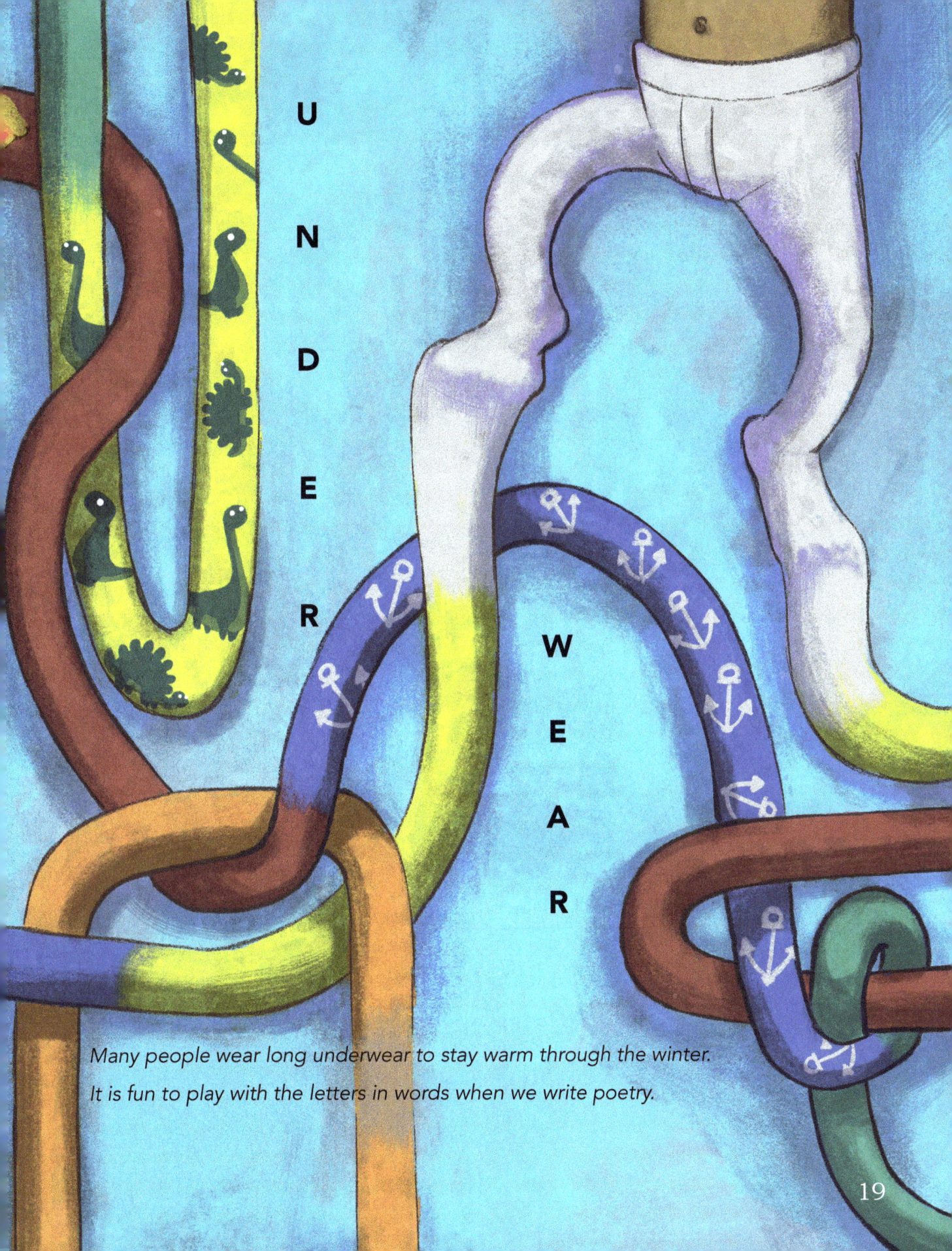

Many people wear long underwear to stay warm through the winter. It is fun to play with the letters in words when we write poetry.

Afraid

When the Northern Lights
put on a show,
people were afraid
a long time ago.

But we know the lights
won't hurt us today,
and it's fun to watch them
while we play.

Dance lights!
Dance away!

A long time ago, the people thought the Northern Lights could come down and hurt them. Today, we know that the lights are both safe and beautiful.

The Call of the Wild

Some kids were never meant
for tables, desks, and chairs,
and when the wild calls to them
they long to be out there.

They love to mush in heavy snow
and feel their bodies climb,
closer to the polar sky
that worries not for time.

They want to hear the husky dogs
howling at the moon,
and watch the northern lights
as they dance to blazing tunes.

Some kids were never meant
to breathe in classroom air,
and when the wild calls to them,
they long to be out there.

Even though it can be cold and dark, many children love the wild freedom of the outdoors in the far north.

Marilyn's Moon Question

I love your name,
but would love it more,
if some extra
O's you wore.

Don't let it end
so fast,
so soon!

Why not change from moon to,

moooooooooooooooooooooooooooooooo
ooooooooooooooooon?

When we write poetry, it is fun to play with words and make them long like I did with mooooooooooooooooooooooooooon.

Joe's Favourite Place

I'm right at the top
of the climbing bars.
When I reach up
I can tickle the stars.

I laugh at the moon,
"You're a butterball!"
And way up there
I'm a part of it all.

I reign as the King
of Arctic nights,
and dance with my queen –
T h e   N o r t h e r n   L i g h t s.

There are climbing bars on the playground. Sometimes, when you are at the top, you feel as if you can touch the stars.

Pack of Wolves

We are playing a game
and it is so much fun,
when Mary yells,
"GET HIM!"
and I start to run.

My friends look like wolves
that are howling at the moon,

Get him!

Get him!
Get him!

a wild haunting tune.

I race through the darkness
as I try to get away,
but they are right behind
in this scary game we play.

I dash to the north
then zig zag to the east.
I try to confuse
that pack of wild beasts.

But they stay on my heels
and give me such a fright,
as I run through the shadows
on this exciting night.

Arctic wolves do not hibernate in the winter. They travel as a pack, and they live and feed together.

It is fun to pretend that a pack of wolves is chasing the boy in this poem.

An Igloo

Cut out blocks
in the snow,
like people did
long ago.

Stack them up
on the ground,
in a circle
round and round.

At the top
shape a dome,
a snowy-roofed
winter home.

A place to hide
till recess ends,
sharing stories
with best friends.

Igloos are used as shelters in emergencies because they can save lives when people are lost or stranded in the snow. When they crawl inside, their bodies heat up the igloo until it is warmer inside than outside.

Love and Honour

Colin, the snowman,
marries Emma,
the snowwoman.

They promise
to love and honour
each other till

they both shall melt.

When the snow is just right, the children make snowmen, snowwomen, and other sculptures on the playground. Many of the ice and snow sculptures are artistic and beautiful.

A Northern Lights Polar Bear

A polar bear is forming
in the lights way up high.

He's growing.
He's spreading.
He's filling up the sky.

He's mammoth.
He's monstrous.
A kid-eating CARNIVORE!

He's swooshing down to eat us!

RIIIIIIIIIIIIIIIIIIIIIIIIIIIIIIIIIIIIIIIIIIIIIING!

We're racing in the door!

The Northern Lights take on images and are often shimmering shades of colours. In this poem, the Northern Lights take on the form of a large polar bear.

There are real polar bears in the far north near water, and they are very dangerous.

Frozen Toes

Ring the bell
really fast.
Our toes are frozen.
They won't last!

They need warmth,
they need sun,

before they snap off
one by one.

Oh no!
Oh no!
Oh no!
Oh no!

Frostbite occurs when it is so cold that the skin freezes. The children are warned to be careful and to stay indoors when it is extremely cold.

Oh no!

Oh no!

Oh no!

Oh no!

Oh no!

Dog Team

We're sculpting our dogs
out of ice and snow
under a moonlit sky.

We're hard at work
but STOP to watch
as a REAL team runs by.

Dog teams are still used in the North because they are safer than snowmobiles. A snowmobile can break down, but the dogs are reliable.

A Recess Chat

Some girls meet in the igloo
to have a recess chat.

They talk about
school
and books
and love
and life
and boys
and kisses

and other things like that.

It is fun to meet with friends and talk during recess. In this poem, the girls find a quiet place to do so inside an igloo on the playground.

My Rabbit Mittens

Through icy winds
and recess storms,
a rabbit's gift
has kept me warm.

The fur and skin of the rabbit are used to make warm mittens. The people of the North always thank the animals for giving their lives so they can be warm.

Gary's Polar Snow Bear

I make a bear
of ice and snow,
and I name him
Snowbear Joe.

He is my friend
all winter long,
and the freezing cold
keeps him strong.

He growls, "I'll stay
and play with you,
until the sky
turns warm and blue."

I make a bear
of ice and snow,
When springtime comes,

Sob!
he'll have to go.

The winters are long, but finally the snow melts, spring comes, and the children's creations of snow and ice begin to disappear.

We Have Light

The season is dark
but there is light,
starlight,
moonlight,
and the whirling dances
of the Great Northern Lights.

Still,

we
wait,
and
wait,
and
wait,
and
wait,
and
wait,

through the long winter night,
for our very first glimpse of

daylight.

Everyone is thrilled when the light returns after the long period of darkness.

ABOUT THE AUTHORS

Kalli Dakos

Kalli Dakos has been delighting her readers with poetry since the release of her best-selling book, *If You're Not Here, Please Raise Your Hand*. She has written six IRA/CBC Children's Choice Selections, such as *Our Principal Promised to Kiss a Pig* and *A Funeral in the Bathroom*.

A former teacher and reading specialist, Dakos taught at Sir Alexander Mackenzie School in Inuvik, Northwest Territories, Canada. She has returned on author visits to encourage the children to write about their fascinating lives above the Arctic Circle. This book was inspired on one of these trips, when "recess in the dark" was chosen as a favourite writing topic.

Dakos frequently celebrates a love of reading in schools all over Canada and the United States, and sometimes as far away as Hong Kong. She has an office in Ogdensburg, New York, and lives in Ottawa, ON, Canada.

Erin Mercer

Erin Mercer is an children's book illustrator currently living in Hantsport, Nova Scotia, Canada, She's inspired by the things she loves the most: cooking, gardening, animals, gaming and travel. Her colourful, whimsical aesthetic focuses on characters and storytelling, and she loves to inject humour into her work. She mixes traditional and digital media, merging her background in fine arts and concept art.

See more from Erin on her website: www.pencilempire.com.

www.ingramcontent.com/pod-product-compliance
Lightning Source LLC
Chambersburg PA
CBHW051320110526
44590CB00031B/4418